Andorra Travel Guide 2025

Epic Itineraries, Scenic Drives, Local

Food & Outdoor Escapes

Daniel M Jernigan

Table of contents

Table of contents

Chapter 1

Welcome to Andorra

Chapter 2

Getting to Andorra Easily

Chapter 3

Getting Around Inside Andorra

Chapter 4

Top Attractions You Can't Miss

Chapter 5

Andorra Itineraries for Every Type of Traveler

Chapter 6

Where to Stay in Andorra

Chapter 7

Where and What to Eat

Chapter 8

Culture, History & Local Life

Chapter 9

Outdoor Adventures & Nature Escapes

Chapter 10
Practical Travel Essentials

Chapter 1

Welcome to Andorra

1.1 Why Andorra Is Europe's BestKept Secret

Tucked between France and Spain in the heart of the Pyrenees, Andorra is one of Europe's smallest yet most captivating countries—a true hidden gem waiting to be explored. Often overlooked on the traditional European travel map, this microstate offers an unrivaled combination of natural beauty, cultural richness, affordability, and safety that sets it apart from better known destinations. With a population of just over 77,000 and a land area of 468 square kilometers, Andorra is where majestic mountains meet medieval villages, and world class ski resorts blend seamlessly with ancient Romanesque churches.

A Country Without an Airport – Yet Incredibly Accessible

One of the things that makes Andorra so fascinating is how it manages to be so accessible despite having no international airport or railway system. Travelers typically arrive via Barcelona (Spain) or Toulouse (France)—both cities offer smooth bus transfers and scenic drives that transform the journey into an adventure of its own. Andorra's relative remoteness has preserved its authentic charm, allowing it to remain largely untouched by the overtourism plaguing other European hotspots.

A Paradise for Nature Lovers and Adventure Seekers

For outdoor enthusiasts, Andorra is nothing short of paradise. Over 90% of its territory is made up of mountains, forests, and lakes, making it a playground for hiking, skiing, snowboarding, mountain biking, and rock climbing. In winter, it's a ski haven with some of the most affordable and expensive ski resorts in Europe, such as Grandvalira and Vallnord. In summer, the snow gives way to lush alpine meadows, inviting travelers to explore UNESCOlisted valleys, pristine lakes, and panoramic viewpoints that rival those of the Alps.

A Cultural Mosaic Hidden in the Mountains

Despite its size, Andorra has a surprisingly rich cultural identity. The country's official language is Catalan, but Spanish, French, and Portuguese are also widely spoken, creating a melting pot of European cultures. Visitors can explore centuries old churches, cobblestone villages like Ordino and Pal, and vibrant festivals that reveal the nation's proud heritage. Add to that its unique co principality system of governance (shared by the President of France and the Bishop of Urgell in Spain), and Andorra stands as a rare example of how ancient traditions and modern democracy can coexist.

Safe, Clean, and Surprisingly Affordable

Andorra enjoys one of the lowest crime rates in the world, making it ideal for solo travelers, families, and retirees alike. Its economy is powered by tourism, banking, and retail—especially duty free shopping, which draws visitors from neighboring countries looking for quality goods at tax free prices. Compared to major cities in Western Europe, the cost of lodging, food, ski passes, and spa treatments in Andorra is often far more affordable, allowing travelers to enjoy a premium experience without a premium price tag.

The Secret is Out—But Still Yours to Discover

Although word is slowly spreading, Andorra has managed to retain its sense of discovery and intimacy. You won't find massive crowds, long lines, or overbooked attractions here. What you will find is a warm welcome, jaw dropping scenery, and a sense of serenity that's increasingly hard to come by in today's world of mass tourism. Whether you come for a weekend of skiing or a two week escape into nature and culture, Andorra offers something rare: a true European adventure that still feels like your personal secret.

1.2 Quick Facts Every Traveler Should Know

Before you step into the captivating landscapes of Andorra, it's helpful to get acquainted with the key facts that will shape your journey. From local currency and climate to language and safety, these quick facts serve as your goto reference to make your travel smooth, informed, and unforgettable.

Location & Geography

Continent: Europe

Region: Eastern Pyrenees, between France and Spain

Area: 468 square kilometers (181 square miles)

Terrain: Mountainous with deep valleys, alpine lakes, and forested slopes

Highest Peak: Coma Pedrosa – 2,942 meters (9,652 feet)

Andorra is a landlocked microstate entirely nestled in the Pyrenees. Its mountainous landscape makes it ideal for winter sports and summer hiking, with over 65 peaks rising above 2,000 meters.
Capital & Cities

Capital: Andorra la Vella (the highest capital city in Europe at 1,023 meters / 3,356 feet)

Major Towns: Escaldes Engordany, Encamp, La Massana, Canillo, Ordino, Sant Julià de Lòria

While Andorra la Vella serves as the cultural and administrative hub, each parish (region) offers its own unique charm—ranging from high altitude ski villages to tranquil countryside retreats.

Language & Communication

Official Language: Catalan

Widely Spoken Languages: Spanish, French, Portuguese

English Use: Spoken in tourist areas, especially hotels, shops, and ski resorts

It's helpful to learn a few Catalan phrases, but most locals in hospitality speak enough English to assist tourists. Multilingual signs and menus are common in popular areas.

Currency & Payments

Currency: Euro (€)

ATMs: Widely available in towns and resorts

Cards: Credit/debit cards are accepted almost everywhere

DutyFree: Yes – Andorra is a tax haven with no VAT

Andorra is a shopper's paradise. From perfumes to electronics and designer fashion, duty free shopping is a big draw. Be aware of customs limits when returning to Spain or France.

Climate & Best Time to Visit

Climate: Alpine climate with cold, snowy winters and mild summers

Winter Season: December to April (ideal for skiing and snowboarding)

Summer Season: June to September (perfect for hiking and nature tours)

Spring & Fall: Quieter, cooler, ideal for peaceful exploration

Skiers flock to the region in winter, while hikers and mountain bikers come for the wildflower trails and lush landscapes in the warmer months.

Time Zone & Electricity

Time Zone: Central European Time (CET), UTC +1 (Daylight Saving Time observed)

Electricity: 230V, 50Hz

Plug Types: Type C and F (European standard two pin plugs)

Travelers from outside Europe may need a plug adapter and voltage converter depending on their home country's system.

Health, Safety & Emergency Services

Emergency Number: 112

Hospitals & Clinics: High Standard medical services available

Water: Safe to drink from taps

Safety: Extremely low crime rate – one of the safest countries in the world

Travel insurance is still recommended, particularly for sports injuries. Pharmacies are well stocked, and English Speaking staff are available in most major centers.

Transportation Overview

No Airports or Rail Stations within Andorra

Main Access Points: Barcelona (Spain), Toulouse (France)

Bus Transfers: Frequent daily services from both cities

Local Transport: Extensive and affordable bus network

Despite lacking an airport or train, Andorra is well connected by modern, comfortable buses that operate year round.

These essential facts not only help you plan better but also give you a cultural and practical foundation before exploring Andorra in depth. As you journey through the mountains, valleys, and villages, you'll find that knowing these little details adds tremendous value to your experience.

1.3 What's New in 2025 for Visitors

Andorra continues to evolve as a premier destination in Europe, offering visitors a blend of natural beauty, cultural richness, and modern amenities. In 2025, several new attractions, events, and initiatives will be introduced to enhance the visitor experience.

Major Events and Festivals

Games of the Small States of Europe

From May 26 to June 1, Andorra la Vella hosted the 2025 Games of the Small States of Europe, welcoming over 800 athletes from nine countries. This multisport event showcases competitions across various disciplines and emphasizes Andorra's commitment to international sports.

Motard Motorcycle Festival

The third edition of Motand, a festival dedicated to motorcycle enthusiasts, takes place from June 27 to 29 at the Canrodes parking area in Santa Coloma. The event features live screenings of the Assen Grand Prix, trial exhibitions, electric motorcycle demos, driving workshops, escape rooms, simulators, and children's activities. Organized routes like the Rider 468 and the Road Trip offer participants scenic journeys through Andorra's landscapes.

Cirque du Soleil Performances

In the summer of 2025, Cirque du Soleil returned to Andorra with a new show, adding a touch of magic and artistry to the country's cultural offerings.

Tourism and Infrastructure Developments

Grandvalira Resort Enhancements

Grandvalira, one of Andorra's premier ski resorts, has invested €20.9 million in upgrades for the 20242025 season. Improvements include enhanced snowmaking systems, the new Estadi Eslalon Creand, and a multifunctional building in Pas de la Casa. Additionally, the resort introduces a new app offering eSIM downloads and real time location tracking on the slopes. Culinary experiences are elevated with Michelin Starred chef Nandu Jubany leading some of the resort's dining establishments.

Sustainable Tourism Initiatives

Andorra is implementing measures to promote sustainable tourism. Efforts include limiting new hotel licenses in oversaturated areas, encouraging luxury accommodations in less visited regions, and investing in renewable energy and efficient water management systems. These initiatives aim to balance tourist influx with environmental preservation.

Adoption of the International Code for the Protection of Tourists

In a move to enhance visitor safety and rights, Andorra has become the 25th country to adhere to the International Code for the Protection of Tourists. This commitment ensures a safer and more ethical environment for travelers, aligning with global standards for tourist protection.

These developments in 2025 reflect Andorra's dedication to offering enriched experiences for its visitors, blending tradition with innovation.

1.4 Essential Travel Tips for FirstTime Visitors

Visiting Andorra for the first time is an exciting experience, but as with any unique destination, a little preparation can go a long way. This landlocked microstate in the Pyrenees may be small, but it offers a wealth of outdoor adventure, cultural charm, and modern comfort. To help you make the most of your trip, here are essential tips that every first time visitor should know.

Pack for the Mountains – Even in Summer

Andorra's weather can change rapidly due to its alpine climate. Even in summer, mornings and evenings can be chilly, especially at higher elevations. Be sure to pack:

Layers of clothing (light and thermal)

Waterproof outerwear (especially in spring and autumn)

Comfortable hiking or walking shoes

Sunscreen and sunglasses (sun is strong at high altitudes)

Gloves, hat, and snow gear (if visiting during winter)

Weather apps are helpful, but always be prepared for sudden changes when venturing into nature.

Understand the Transport Logistics

Andorra does not have an airport or railway station. Most visitors arrive via:

BarcelonaEl Prat Airport (Spain) or ToulouseBlagnac Airport (France)

From either, buses take you through a scenic 34 hour journey to Andorra la Vella or other towns

Once in the country, the local bus network is excellent and affordable. Car rentals are available, but winter visitors should ensure their vehicle is snow ready (chains or winter tires required by law between November and April).

Currency and Payments – No Surprises Here

Andorra uses the Euro (€) even though it is not a member of the European Union. Here's what to know:

Credit/debit cards are widely accepted, including contactless payments

ATMs are easy to find in towns and shopping areas

Andorra is a duty free zone, making it an excellent place to buy perfumes, electronics, alcohol, and luxury goods at lower prices

However, note that customs limits apply when returning to France or Spain—be mindful of your receipts and packing

Language and Communication Tips

The official language is Catalan, but Spanish and French are commonly spoken. English is also widely used in tourist zones.

Learning a few Catalan greetings (e.g., Bon dia for "Good morning") is appreciated

Road signs and menus are usually multilingual

Free WiFi is common in hotels and cafes

EU visitors can use EU roaming, but others should check roaming rates or get a local eSIM via the Grandvalira app or telecom providers

Safety, Health, and Insurance

Andorra is one of the safest countries in the world. Crime is rare, and the atmosphere is calm and family friendly.

Emergency number: 112 (for police, ambulance, or fire services)

Healthcare is high quality, but travel insurance is recommended, especially for winter sports injuries

Pharmacies are well stocked and easy to find, often with multilingual staff

Tap water is safe to drink and often comes straight from the mountains

Respect Local Laws and Customs

Andorra is a respectful and eco conscious society. Keep in mind:

Littering is frowned upon – use recycling bins and clean up after hiking

Quiet hours are generally observed after 10 p.m. in residential areas

Smoking is banned in enclosed public spaces and restaurants

When visiting churches and historic sites, dress modestly

Download Helpful Travel Apps

A few apps to make your Andorran journey smoother:

Andbus – For airport shuttles and transfers

Moovit – To track local bus lines and schedules

Grandvalira or Vallnord Apps – For ski pass management, live maps, and weather

Google Translate – For instant communication

Whether you're skiing, shopping, hiking, or simply relaxing in a thermal spa, these tips will help you blend in with locals and make the most of your stay in Andorra. First Time visitors often become lifelong fans—and with good reason.

Chapter 2

Getting to Andorra Easily

2.1 Airports, Border Crossings, and Access Routes

Andorra is nestled high in the Pyrenees, surrounded entirely by France to the north and Spain to the south. It has no airport or train station, but don't let that discourage you—access is remarkably efficient and incredibly scenic. Understanding the main gateways and how to navigate them is the first step to planning your perfect Andorran adventure.

No Airport, No Problem

Though Andorra lacks its own international airport, it is easily accessible from major airports in nearby cities:

Barcelona–El Prat Airport (Spain) – Approx. 200 km (125 miles)

Toulouse–Blagnac Airport (France) – Approx. 185 km (115 miles)

Girona–Costa Brava Airport (Spain) – Approx. 160 km (100 miles)

These airports offer connections to most major cities in Europe and beyond. Once you land, the rest of the journey is done by comfortable intercity buses, car rental, or private transfers.

Main Border Crossings into Andorra

There are only two official road entry points:

From Spain: Via the CG1 highway, through the town of La Farga de Moles (near La Seu d'Urgell)

From France: Via the RN22 and CG2, crossing at Pas de la Casa, near the French town of L'Hospitaletprèsl'Andorre

Both crossings are open year round, although snow and ice may affect the French side during winter—making the Spanish route more reliable in harsh weather conditions.

Driving to Andorra

Whether you rent a car or bring your own, the roads to Andorra are well maintained and scenic, with dramatic mountain views. Here's what to keep in mind:

Tolls: Spanish and French highways may have tolls. Keep some cash or a credit card handy.

Parking: Abundant in towns and ski resorts, with multilevel garages in Andorra la Vella.

Snow Requirements: From November 1 to May 15, winter tires or snow chains are mandatory by law when entering Andorra or driving within its borders.

Fuel: Gas is cheaper in Andorra than in France or Spain, making it a good spot to fill up.

2.2 Best Ways to Enter from France and Spain

Whether you're coming from France or Spain, both routes offer a unique travel experience. Here's a breakdown of the most popular and reliable options depending on your departure point and travel preferences.

Entering from Spain

Spain offers the most direct and reliable route to Andorra, especially in winter.

Option 1: From Barcelona

By Bus: Multiple companies, such as Andbus and Directbus, run regular routes from both Terminals 1 and 2 at Barcelona Airport directly to Andorra la Vella. Travel time: approx. 3 to 4 hours.

By Car: Rent a car from Barcelona and take the C16 highway through Manresa and La Seu d'Urgell. Scenic and smooth, this route is preferred for those who enjoy flexibility.

Option 2: From Lleida or La Seu d'Urgell

Lleida has a high speed train station connecting to major Spanish cities. From there, buses and taxis take you to Andorra via La Seu d'Urgell.

La Seu d'Urgell is the closest Spanish town to the Andorran border (just 10 km away).

Best For: Smooth roads, fewer winter closures, quick access to southern Andorra towns and the capital.

Entering from France

The French route is stunning, winding through alpine passes, but can be challenging in winter due to snow.

Option 1: From Toulouse

By Bus: Regular daily buses from Toulouse Airport and city center to Andorra, offered by companies like Andbus and Novatel. Travel time: approx. 3.5 to 4.5 hours.

By Car: Take the A66 highway south toward AxlesThermes, then follow the RN20 and RN22 toward the Pas de la Casa border.

Option 2: From Foix or L'Hospitalet

L'Hospitaletprèsl'Andorre has a train station that connects to major French cities.

From there, taxis or buses take you the final leg through the mountains to Pas de la Casa.

Best For: Access to eastern Andorra (Pas de la Casa ski resort), scenic mountain views, and travelers coming from northern France or central Europe.

Things to Keep in Mind

Travel Insurance: Highly recommended, especially if you plan on skiing or driving in winter.

Documentation: No visa is required for EU citizens. Travelers from nonSchengen countries must hold a Schengen visa to enter Andorra via France or Spain.

Customs Checks: Andorra is not in the EU Customs Union. Border agents may check your bags, especially if you've done significant duty free shopping.

No matter which way you come, the journey to Andorra is an adventure in itself—winding roads, towering peaks, and breathtaking views await at every turn. In the next section, we'll look at the best travel itineraries to match your time and interests in the country.

2.3 Visa, Passport & Entry Requirements

Although Andorra is not a member of the European Union or the Schengen Area, it maintains an open border policy with its neighbors, France and Spain. This means that you cannot fly directly into

Andorra—you must pass through one of these two countries first. Therefore, the visa requirements for Andorra depend entirely on your eligibility to enter the Schengen zone.

Entry Requirements Overview

Passport Validity: All travelers must carry a valid passport. It should be valid for at least three months beyond the date of departure from the Schengen Area.

National ID Cards: Citizens of EU or EEA countries can enter using a national identity card. No visa is required.

NonEU Travelers: If you're from a country that requires a visa to enter France or Spain (e.g., India, South Africa, China), you'll need a multiple entry Schengen visa, as you will re enter France or Spain after visiting Andorra.

Important Notes

No Border Control into Andorra: You won't find traditional passport control when entering or leaving Andorra by road, but authorities may conduct checks, especially during peak seasons or holidays.

Customs Declarations: Andorra is a duty free zone. Customs checks are often enforced when returning to France or Spain to prevent smuggling of goods like alcohol, tobacco, or electronics beyond allowable limits.

No Visa Issued by Andorra: Since there's no airport or border crossing independent of Spain or France, Andorra does not issue its own visas. Entry is entirely dependent on your right to enter the Schengen Area.

Quick Summary by Region

Before your trip, check with your embassy or consulate for the most uptodate information based on your nationality.

2.4 Budget and Luxury Travel Options to Arrive

Andorra may be a secluded mountain escape, but reaching it can be tailored to suit any travel budget—from backpackers to luxury seekers. Whether you're saving on every euro or looking to arrive in alpine style, here's how to plan your journey to match your travel goals.

Budget Travel Options

🚌 Bus Transfers (Most Affordable Option)

The most popular and wallet friendly way to reach Andorra is by bus from nearby airports such as Barcelona, Girona, or Toulouse.

Services like Andbus, Directbus, and Alsa offer frequent, comfortable buses with onboard WiFi and luggage storage.

Cost: €30–€45 one way

Best For: Backpackers, solo travelers, and families on a budget

🚆 Train + Shuttle Combo (Via France)

Take a train to L'Hospitaletprèsl'Andorre (from Toulouse or Paris), then connect via a local shuttle or taxi to Pas de la Casa.

A scenic, slow route ideal for those who prefer trains over long bus rides.

Cost: €15–€25 for the train + €10–€20 for the shuttle

Best For: Travelers exploring southern France, train enthusiasts

🚗 Carpooling & Rideshare Apps

Use services like BlaBlaCar to find rides from Barcelona or Toulouse to Andorra.

Often cheaper and faster than public buses, especially when booked at the last minute.

Cost: €15–€25

Best For: Young travelers, eco conscious adventurers

MidRange to Luxury Travel Options

🚐 Private Transfers

Door To Door airport pickups in comfortable SUVs or vans, with space for luggage and ski gear.

Often include bilingual drivers and optional extras like stopovers for sightseeing.

Cost: €150–€300 depending on group size

Best For: Groups, business travelers, families with kids

🚁 Helicopter Transfers (Yes, Really!)

Available from Barcelona and Toulouse, helicopter charters offer an unforgettable entry over the Pyrenees.

Land directly in Andorra la Vella or ski resort helipads, avoiding traffic altogether.

Cost: Starting at €2,000+ per flight (up to 4 passengers)

Best For: VIPs, couples on luxury holidays, time sensitive travelers

🚗 Premium Car Rentals

Rent high end vehicles (e.g., 4x4 SUVs, luxury sedans) from major cities and drive in.

Roads are well paved, and the journey is scenic—especially from Spain.

Addons: GPS, winter tires, ski racks

Cost: €70–€150 per day

Best For: Independent luxury travelers, photographers, explorers

Whether you're seeking value or indulgence, getting to Andorra is part of the adventure. From budget buses winding through mountain passes to helicopter flights soaring over the peaks, there's a travel style here for everyone.

Chapter 3

Getting Around Inside Andorra

Despite its small size, Andorra offers a surprisingly efficient and scenic transportation experience. From navigating winding alpine roads to hopping on a reliable network of buses and shuttles, getting around the country is part of the adventure. Whether you're exploring quaint villages or heading up to a mountaintop spa, this chapter will equip you with everything you need to know about internal travel in Andorra.

3.1 Public Transportation: Buses, Shuttles & Tips

Andorra's public transport system is compact but efficient, affordable, and clean. Since there are no railways or domestic flights, buses are the primary mode of public transport—and they work remarkably well for tourists.

Bus Network Overview

Andorra's bus system, locally known as Interurbana, connects most towns and parishes, as well as popular attractions, ski resorts, and hiking zones. The services are numbered from L1 to L6, and additional tourist or ski shuttles are available seasonally.

L1 (Andorra la Vella – Sant Julià de Lòria)

L2 (Andorra la Vella – Encamp – Canillo)

L3 (Andorra la Vella – Ordino – Arcalís)

L4 (Andorra la Vella – La Massana – Pal/Arinsal)

L5 (Andorra la Vella – Encamp – Grau Roig)

L6 (Andorra la Vella – Pas de la Casa)

Frequencies range from every 20–60 minutes during the day, with fewer services at night or on weekends.

Tickets and Pricing

Bus fares are reasonable:

Short rides: €1.90–€3.00

Longer trips across the country: €4.00–€6.85

Travel Pass: The Targeta 10/45 is a rechargeable card offering 10 trips for €8–€18 depending on zones. You can purchase and top up at kiosks or online.

Some buses offer contactless payment, while others require cash. Always carry a few coins just in case.

Airport and Ski Shuttles

Special buses and shuttles run to/from:

Barcelona and Toulouse Airports: Andbus, Novatel, and Directbus

Ski Resorts: Grandvalira and Vallnord shuttle buses (free for ski pass holders during season)

During peak season (December to March), booking your shuttle in advance is highly recommended.

Travel Tips for Public Transport

Download the Mou_T_B app for live schedules, maps, and route planning.

Buses don't run 24/7. Most services end by 9:00–10:00 PM.

Stop on request. Some rural stops require you to wave down the driver.

Luggage is allowed but limited—ideal for day trips or light travel.

Most drivers speak Catalan, Spanish, or French, but basic English is understood in tourist areas.

Public transport is perfect for eco conscious travelers, day trippers, and those staying in central towns. However, if you're exploring remote valleys or plan to move quickly, renting a car might offer more freedom.

3.2 Renting a Car: Mountain Roads & Safety

Driving in Andorra can be one of the highlights of your trip. The mountain roads here offer unmatched scenic beauty, and with no road tolls and inexpensive fuel, self driving is a smart and flexible option for many travelers.

Where to Rent

Car rentals are available in Andorra la Vella, Encamp, and at airport cities like Barcelona and Toulouse. If you're starting from outside Andorra, consider:

Renting in Spain for better prices and automatic vehicles

Choosing 4x4s or SUVs in winter for safety and road clearance

Booking early during ski season or summer holidays

Top rental agencies include Europcar, Avis, Hertz, and local operators like Autorent and Andocar.

Driving Requirements

License: EU licenses are accepted. NonEU visitors should bring an International Driving Permit (IDP).

Minimum age: 21–25 depending on company

Insurance: Basic coverage is included, but add snow and tire protection during winter

Navigation: GPS rental is offered, but using offline maps or apps like Waze or Google Maps is more reliable

Road Safety & Mountain Driving Tips

Driving in the Pyrenees is both rewarding and challenging. Here's what to expect:

Road Conditions

Main roads (CG1–CG6) are well maintained and paved

Secondary roads to remote villages may be steep or narrow

In winter (Nov–Apr), snow and ice are common—snow chains or winter tires are mandatory by law

Mountain Driving Essentials

Use low gears when descending steep roads to avoid brake overheating

Watch for hairpin turns and sharp switchbacks, especially near ski resorts

Pull over at scenic lookouts—many have safe parking areas

Avoid night driving in unfamiliar terrain due to limited lighting

Fuel and Parking

Fuel is cheaper than in Spain or France, making Andorra a great spot to fill up

Fuel stations are plentiful in cities, rare in villages—don't wait until the last minute

Parking in towns ranges from free village lots to metered garages in Andorra la Vella (€1–€2/hour)

Renting a car gives you the freedom to chase waterfalls, drive to high altitude trails, or stop for lunch in a hidden alpine village—at your pace.

3.3 Apps & Tools for HassleFree Navigation

Modern travelers have a powerful edge—smart tools that turn complex itineraries into smooth experiences. Whether you're using public transport or navigating the highlands, here are the best apps and tools to simplify your travel inside Andorra.

Navigation and Route Planning

Google Maps & Waze

Ideal for driving and walking routes

Offers traffic updates, speed limit alerts, and estimated travel times

Waze is particularly helpful for mountain road hazards and real time alerts

Moovit

Great for public transport planning

Provides real time bus arrival info, route suggestions, and alerts

Komoot & AllTrails

Best for hiking, cycling, and mountain trail navigation

Includes offline maps, elevation data, and trail reviews

Local & Government Travel Apps

Mou_T_B

Official Andorran mobility app

Covers bus lines, stops, and service alerts

Supports multilingual search and offline use

Grandvalira & Vallnord Apps

For ski season visitors

Show live snow conditions, ski lift wait times, slope maps, and epass management

Andbus / Novatel

Airport transfer and ski shuttle management

Offers online booking, etickets, and real time bus location tracking

Emergency & Safety

112 Andorra App

Emergency alerts and contact options

Geolocation helps rescuers reach you in mountain areas

Offers updates on avalanche risks, road closures, and weather events

Weather Apps (Meteo.ad, AccuWeather)

Accurate mountain forecasts

Check before hikes or drives—weather changes fast at altitude

Bonus Tools

Google Translate or iTranslate – Useful for Catalan menus or road signs

XE Currency Converter – Check the value of duty free shopping in real time

Booking.com & Maps.me – Great for navigating to your accommodation

By using these tools before and during your trip, you'll avoid delays, stay informed, and unlock local insights with just a few taps.

3.4 Scenic Drives and Local Transit Routes

Some of the most unforgettable moments in Andorra happen between destinations. With its dramatic mountain terrain, lush valleys, and medieval villages, driving through Andorra is like cruising through a postcard. Whether you're behind the wheel or on a bus, here are the most scenic and practical routes to explore.

Top Scenic Drives

Andorra la Vella → Ordino → Arcalís (Route CG3)

A beautiful ride through forests and mountain vistas

Highlights: Museu Postal, Ordino village, and VallnordArcalís ski area

Ideal in autumn when the trees glow golden

Encamp → Canillo → Pas de la Casa (Route CG2)

This route climbs into the clouds and delivers stunning views of the Grandvalira resort area

Stop at the Tibetan Bridge in Canillo and the Sanctuary of Meritxell

Continue east to Pas de la Casa for high altitude shopping or skiing

La Massana → Pal → Arinsal (CG4)

Narrow but thrilling road that hugs the mountain

Access to VallnordPal/Arinsal, with cafes and mountain biking trails

Fantastic in summer for panoramic views and hiking trailheads

Encamp → Grau Roig → Port d'Envalira

The highest paved road in the Pyrenees, rising above 2,400m

Breathtaking snowfields in winter, wildflower meadows in summer

Take it slow—this drive is all about the views

Best Bus Routes for Travelers Without a Car

L3 (Andorra la Vella – Ordino – Arcalís): See rural Andorra with ease

L5 (Andorra la Vella – Encamp – Grau Roig): Ideal for skiing or hiking in Grandvalira

Tourist Bus (June–September): A hoponhopoffplus route that visits major sites like Sant Joan de Caselles, Romanesque churches, and valley viewpoints

Seasonal Tips for Scenic Travel

Summer: Mountain roads are dry and fully accessible—perfect for drives, hikes, and photo ops

Autumn: Fewer crowds and brilliant foliage

Winter: Snow Covered peaks offer a magical backdrop, but require extra caution on the roads

Spring: Melting snow feeds waterfalls—ideal for nature drives and riverside stops

Andorra may only be 468 km^2, but its terrain is rich with contrasts—deep valleys, jagged peaks, serene forests, and bustling towns. Each drive tells its own story.

Navigating Andorra is part of the magic. Whether you're relying on buses, renting a car, or combining both, you'll find the country easy to explore, surprisingly efficient, and always scenic. Use public transport to mingle with locals, take control with your own vehicle, and lean on smart apps to unlock every hidden corner.

Chapter 4

Top Attractions You Can't Miss

Despite its small size, Andorra is brimming with spectacular sights, thrilling outdoor activities, and serene spots that draw in visitors year round. This chapter highlights the most iconic and unmissable attractions, from towering ski resorts and UNESCOlisted valleys to futuristic thermal spas and breathtaking skywalks.

4.1 Grandvalira & Vallnord Ski Resorts

Andorra is a paradise for winter sports lovers, boasting some of the most well developed ski resorts in Europe. Two massive ski domains dominate the country's alpine landscape: Grandvalira and Vallnord. Together, they offer over

300 km of slopes, stateoftheart facilities, and a season that often stretches from late November to early April.

Grandvalira Ski Resort

Size: Over 210 km of interconnected ski runs

Zones: Includes Encamp, Canillo, El Tarter, Soldeu, Grau Roig, and Pas de la Casa

Best for: Intermediate to advanced skiers, snowboarding, families

Highlights:

High Speed lifts and gondolas

Snow parks, freestyle zones, and FIS World Cup tracks

Beginner slopes and ski schools

Night skiing and aprèsski bars

You can ski in the morning, relax in a spa by afternoon, and dine on mountaintop terraces by evening. Soldeu and El Tarter are especially popular for luxury stays and scenic views.

Vallnord Pal Arinsal & Ordino Arcalís

VallnordPal Arinsal: Linked ski areas suited for beginners and families

Ordino Arcalís: Known for powder snow and backcountry skiing

Best for:

Beginners, kids, and those looking to learn

Freeride skiing and splitboarding

Why Visit:

Less crowded than Grandvalira

Offers panoramic trails, ski bike rentals, and snowshoeing

Great summer base for mountain biking and hiking

Even outside ski season, these resorts transform into adventure parks with zip lining, via ferrata climbs, and alpine coaster rides.

4.2 Madriu Perafita Claror Valley (UNESCO Site)

This sprawling glacial valley—recognized as a UNESCO World Heritage Site—is one of Andorra's greatest treasures. Spanning nearly 10% of the country, the MadriuPerafitaClaror Valley is a haven of highaltitude lakes, stone shepherd huts, pine forests, and remote mountain trails.

Why It's Special

Designated a Cultural Landscape by UNESCO for its preserved pastoral traditions

No roads or development inside the valley—only footpaths and mule trails

Offers a rare glimpse of preindustrial Pyrenean life

Popular Activities

Hiking and trekking: Wellmarked GR (Grande Randonnée) routes take you past ruins, waterfalls, and wildlife

Photography: Crystal Clear glacial lakes and ridgeline vistas

Picnicking and camping: Remote bivouac spots with stargazing potential

Access Points

Escaldes Engordany trailhead (closest to Andorra la Vella)

Ràmio or Entremesaigües for short 12 hour hikes

For longer hikes, use Refugi de l'Illa as a base camp (requires moderate fitness)

Tips

Visit in late spring to early autumn for snow free trails

Wear solid hiking boots and bring water/snacks

Download trail maps offline—cell signal is limited

Whether you're trekking solo or on a guided ecotour, the Madriu Valley provides a tranquil escape into nature and history.

4.3 Caldea Thermal Spa Experience

Step into another dimension at Caldea, Andorra's largest and most iconic thermal spa complex, located in EscaldesEngordany. With its futuristic glass spire towering above the city, Caldea offers relaxation with a dramatic flair.

What to Expect

Over 6,000 m² of thermal pools, saunas, hammams, and wellness spaces

Sourced from natural sulfur rich hot springs

A mix of Icelandic, Roman, and Asian Inspired spa zones

Top Facilities:

Indoor and outdoor lagoons with mountain views

Icelandic baths, water beds, and heated marble slabs

Hydromassage stations, waterfalls, and vapor rooms

Panoramic terraces for relaxation

Caldea for Everyone

Thermoludique: The main spa, suitable for ages 5+ (great for families)

Inúu: The adults only premium section with more exclusive services

Likids: Spa just for kids (ages 3–8), with supervision and play areas

Wellness Extras

Book a massage, facial, or holistic treatment

Combine spa time with lunch or dinner at Blu Restaurant, which offers Mediterranean cuisine with thermal water views

Night spa sessions (with light shows) are a highlight for couples

Pro tip: Book tickets online to secure your entry and skip the queue, especially during weekends or winter holidays.

4.4 Mirador Roc del Quer Skywalk & Views

Few places in Europe offer a better vantage point than the Mirador Roc del Quer, a jaw dropping skywalk suspended over a 500 meter drop into the valley below. Located near Canillo, this modern viewpoint has become a must visit landmark for both adrenaline seekers and landscape lovers.

The Experience

A 12 meter long glass roofed platform juts out from the cliffside

At the edge, you'll meet a striking bronze sculpture of a contemplative man gazing into the valley—a symbol of harmony between man and nature

Panoramic views of the Valira d'Orient Valley, the Pyrenees, and nearby peaks like Pic de Casamanya

Getting There

Just a 10 minute drive from Canillo

Ample parking and a short walking path from the lot

Wheelchair Accessible route and informative panels in English, French, Spanish, and Catalan

Best Times to Visit

Sunrise and sunset for dramatic lighting and fewer crowds

Late spring to early autumn for clear skies and comfortable weather

Nearby Attractions

Combine your visit with stops at:

Sant Joan de Caselles Church (11th century Romanesque gem)

Camillo's Tibetan Bridge – one of Europe's longest pedestrian suspension bridges

Valle de Incles – perfect for a scenic hike or picnic after the viewpoint

Photography Tips

Bring a wide angle lens or use panorama mode

Use a neutral density filter if shooting at midday

Drones are permitted but must follow Andorra's drone regulations (check before flying)

Andorra's top attractions offer an impressive mix of adrenaline, nature, wellness, and cultural wonder. Whether you're carving through powder at Grandvalira, soaking in Caldea's thermal pools, or gazing across valleys from the Roc del Quer, every experience here is memorable and immersive.

Chapter 5

Andorra Itineraries for Every Type of Traveler

Andorra may be small, but it offers a surprising variety of experiences packed into its mountainous terrain. Whether you're visiting for a quick weekend escape or planning a twoweek immersion, this chapter provides curated itineraries for every type of traveler—from nature lovers and history buffs to spa seekers and thrillchasers. You'll also find seasonal suggestions that maximize the best of each time of year.

5.1 3 Day Quick Tour Highlights

Perfect for weekend travelers, business stopovers, or a scenic detour from Spain or France, this 3day Andorra itinerary packs in the essentials for a memorable short trip.

Day 1: Arrival and Relaxation

Arrive via Barcelona or Toulouse, transfer to Andorra by shuttle or rental car

Check into a hotel in Andorra la Vella or Escaldes Engordany

Explore the historic old quarter (Barri Antic) and visit the Casa de la Vall

Evening soak at Caldea Thermal Spa

Dinner at Restaurant Versailles or Platinum

Day 2: Culture and Mountains

Morning visit to Sant Joan de Caselles church (Romanesque architecture)

Ride to Mirador Roc del Quer for stunning views

Afternoon hike or drive in Incles Valley

Optional evening shopping at Andorra 2000 or Pyrénées Department Store

Day 3: Choose Your Adventure

Winter: Half Day skiing in Grandvalira (Soldeu/El Tarter)

Spring/Summer: Short hike in MadriuPerafitaClaror Valley

Lunch with views at Borda Vella or L'Ovella Negra

Depart for Barcelona/Toulouse by late afternoon

5.2 7 Day Adventure Explorer Plan

This one week itinerary is ideal for those seeking a balance of adventure, culture, and relaxation. It includes top attractions, outdoor fun, and hidden gems.

Day 1: Arrival & Capital Discovery

Arrive and settle into Andorra la Vella

Explore museums like Carmen Thyssen or Perfume Museum

Stroll the capital's pedestrian shopping streets

Dinner at El Refugi Alpí (local specialties)

Day 2: Grandvalira Skiing or Summer Biking

Full day in Grandvalira (skiing, snowboarding, or biking in summer)

Lunch on the mountain at CBbC Soldeu

Aprèsski or spa time at Inúu Spa

Day 3: Eastern Valleys Exploration

Drive to Ordino, stop at the Casa de Areny Plandolit Museum

Continue to Sorteny Natural Park for hiking and picnic

Dinner in La Cort de Popaire (typical Andorran borda)

Day 4: Culture & Spiritual Sites

Visit Santuario de Meritxell, Andorra's national sanctuary

Drive scenic mountain routes past Encamp and Canillo

Visit Sant Miquel d'Engolasters and Lake Engolasters

Day 5: Vallnord Adventures

Summer: Ziplining, mountain karting in Pal Arinsal Adventure Park

Winter: Ski or snow activities at Vallnord PalArinsal

Dinner in Erts or La Massana

Day 6: UNESCO Heritage Hike

Trek into the MadriuPerafitaClaror Valley

Picnic near Refugi de Fontvert

Return to Escaldes and enjoy a quiet evening meal

Day 7: Souvenirs and Departure

Morning free for shopping or one last café stop

Depart via shared transfer or rental car

5.3 14 Day Full Immersion Itinerary

For travelers wanting a deep dive into Andorra's culture, cuisine, history, and nature, this two week itinerary leaves no corner unexplored.

Week 1: Cultural Foundations & Natural Beauty

Day 1–2: Arrival and Andorra la Vella

Explore the capital, Caldea Spa, and old town

Day trip to Engolasters Lake & Trails

Day 3: Museums & Villages

Visit Ordino, La Massana, and Casa Cristo Ethnographic Museum

Day 4–5: Incles & Vall d'Incles

Base in Soldeu

Multi Day hiking loop with overnight mountain hut stay (Refugi de Juclà)

Day 6: Relax & Recover

Spa day at Anyós Park

Optional wine tasting or chocolate tour

Day 7: Churches & Romanesque Art

Visit Sant Martí de la Cortinada, Sant Climent de Pal

Guided Romanesque route tour

Week 2: Adventures, Wellness & Hidden Valleys

Day 8–9: Grandvalira or Vallnord

Choose adventure activities (skiing, biking, ziplining)

Include an adventure guide or group excursion

Day 10–11: MadriuPerafitaClaror Valley Trek

Deep hiking into UNESCO site

Stay in Refugi de l'Illa or Camp de Claror

Day 12: Local Life in Canillo & Encamp

Ride Funicamp cable car

Shop for local cheese, jam, and wine

Day 13: Miradors and Final Views

Drive through Port d'Envalira, highest paved road in the Pyrenees

Visit Mirador del Collet de Montaup and Roc del Quer

Day 14: Depart with Full Heart

Last stroll through old quarters, breakfast in a patisserie

Transfer out

5.4 Seasonal Routes: Winter, Spring, Summer, Fall

Andorra is a year round destination. Here's how to tailor your trip for each season.

Winter (Dec–Mar): Snow Sports Paradise

Ski in Grandvalira or Vallnord

Ride snowmobiles or dog sleds in La Rabassa

Cozy spa nights at Caldea

Hot wine at winter markets

Ideal Base: Soldeu, Canillo, or Escaldes

Spring (Apr–May): Blossoms and Hiking

Hike Madriu Valley or Sorteny Nature Park

Visit mountain villages and wildflower meadows

Celebrate Easter and spring festivals

Ideal Base: Ordino or La Massana

Summer (Jun–Aug): Adventure Playground

Mountain biking in Pal Bike Park

Kayaking or paddleboarding at Engolasters Lake

Attend Andorra la Vella Music Festival

Perfect time for high altitude treks

Ideal Base: El Tarter or Incles Valley

Fall (Sept–Nov): Culture and Color

Enjoy golden forests in Comapedrosa Nature Park

Try cider and game dishes in local restaurants

Visit churches and Romanesque routes without crowds

Ideal Base: Anyós or Encamp

From quick highlights to immersive adventures, these itineraries ensure that every traveler—regardless of time or season—experiences the best of Andorra. With thoughtful planning and the flexibility to adapt based on weather and interests, your trip can be both spontaneous and deeply fulfilling.

Chapter 6

Where to Stay in Andorra

Choosing where to stay in Andorra is a key part of shaping your travel experience. Whether you're seeking luxury in the capital, a rustic chalet in the mountains, or a budget friendly base for skiing, Andorra offers a range of accommodations that cater to every traveler. This chapter explores the best places to rest your head, categorized by style, location, and budget.

6.1 Hotels in Andorra la Vella & Escaldes

The capital city, Andorra la Vella, and the neighboring town of EscaldesEngordany form the country's bustling urban heart. Here, you'll find a wide selection of hotels perfect for shoppers, business travelers, spa lovers, and first time visitors.

Why Stay Here?

Central location with access to shopping districts, restaurants, museums, and spas

Easy public transportation to ski resorts and rural valleys

Great for short visits and cultural immersion

Top Hotel Picks

Andorra Park Hotel (5star): A luxury retreat hidden behind lush gardens with panoramic views, indoor and outdoor pools, and wellness facilities.

Hotel Plaza (5star): Opulent interiors, gourmet dining, and walking distance to major shopping streets.

Hotel Roc Blanc (4star): Attached to the Roc Blanc Spa and near Caldea, ideal for wellness weekends.

Acta Arthotel (4star): Contemporary rooms, riverfront views, and a reputation for superb service.

Good for:

Couples looking for spa and relaxation

Shoppers targeting Avenida Meritxell duty free zones

Culture lovers wanting access to museums and historic sites

Travel Tip:

Book in advance for winter or summer weekends—these hotels fill fast during peak holiday seasons and festivals.

6.2 Cozy Chalets & Boutique Inns

For a more authentic, intimate, and romantic stay, head to Andorra's alpine villages where stone chalets and boutique inns offer peace and mountain charm. These accommodations are particularly popular with couples, nature lovers, and digital nomads seeking quiet retreats.

Top Locations

Ordino: A picturesque village surrounded by forests and nature parks

La Massana: Great blend of local life and access to trails or ski lifts

Canillo & Incles Valley: Ideal for hiking, serenity, and dramatic alpine views

Best Picks

Hotel Mu (Ordino): Rustic design with modern amenities and mountain views

Abba Xalet Suites (Sispony): Stone Built chalet with spa and pool in summer

Hotel Naudi Boutique (Soldeu): Adultsonly retreat with a focus on elegance, local cuisine, and views of the slopes

El Serrat Chalet Hotel: Quiet and cozy, perfect for exploring Sorteny Valley

Why Choose a Chalet Stay?

More privacy and charm than chain hotels

Warm hospitality and homemade breakfasts

Often located near hiking trails, ski lifts, or viewpoints

Pro tip: These are especially beautiful in autumn, when the valleys light up with fall colors.

6.3 Budget Hostels & Family Guesthouses

Andorra is very friendly to budget conscious travelers, families, and backpackers. From basic but clean dorms to family run pensions, the country has a solid network of affordable stays.

Best Areas for Budget Accommodation

Encamp: Strategic base for both hiking and skiing via Funicamp cable car

La Massana: Budgetfriendly and close to Vallnord access

Pas de la Casa: Right on the border with France, with cheap ski hostels

Top Picks

Albergue Pension Barri Antic (Andorra la Vella): Cozy, centrally located hostel with shared and private rooms.

Mountain Hostel Tarter: High End feel on a budget; great social vibe, shared kitchen, and hot tub.

Hotel Cims Pas de la Casa: Excellent for skiers; basic rooms with views and ski lockers.

Hotel Encamp: Affordable and functional, with free ski bus and breakfast options.

Great For:

Solo travelers and digital nomads

Budget adventurers or ski enthusiasts

Families looking for friendly, low cost lodging

Tip:

Most hostels and guesthouses provide free WiFi, lockers, and sometimes kitchen access—perfect for saving on meals.

6.4 Mountain Lodges for Ski & Nature Lovers

Mountain lodges and refugees (mountain huts) provide a unique and immersive way to experience the wild side of Andorra. These accommodations offer proximity to nature and a base for skiing, trekking, or alpine adventures.

Types of Lodges

Luxury ski lodges near Soldeu and Arcalís

Familyrun alpine inns with fireplaces and rustic menus

Refugis for hikers—simple, communal lodging high in the mountains

Top Recommendations

Sport Hotel Hermitage & Spa (Soldeu): One of Andorra's finest ski lodges, combining 5 star elegance with direct access to slopes and a massive wellness center.

Hotel Grau Roig Boutique & Spa: Isolated luxury with gourmet dining, wood interiors, and skiin/ski out access.

Refugi de Sorteny: Newly renovated hut in the heart of Sorteny Valley, great for hiking or snowshoeing.

Refugi de l'Illa: Remote stone lodge for serious trekkers exploring the Madriu Valley.

Benefits

Wake up right on the slopes or trailheads

Often include gear rentals, lift tickets, or guides

Some offer half board with traditional Andorran meals

Important: Mountain huts like Refugi de Juclà and Refugi Borda de Sorteny require advance booking, especially during peak hiking months (June to September).

Whether you prefer a luxury suite with spa indulgences or a cozy mountain hut under the stars,

Andorra offers the perfect place to stay for every traveler and season. Use your accommodation choice to complement your itinerary, choosing locations that enhance your activities and interests.

Chapter 7

Where and What to Eat

One of the most enjoyable ways to experience Andorra is through its food. Nestled between France and Spain, Andorran cuisine is a rich blend of Catalan, Occitan, and mountain influences. From hearty stews served in rustic mountain bordas (stone farmhouses) to gourmet plates in upscale restaurants, this chapter will guide you through what to eat and where to find it. Whether you're a meat lover, vegan, or street food explorer, Andorra has something for every palate.

7.1 Traditional Andorran Dishes to Try

Andorran food is warm, rich, and deeply rooted in its mountain heritage. The cuisine often features locally sourced ingredients, such as wild game, mushrooms, cheese, trout, and seasonal vegetables. Here are a few must try dishes during your visit:

Escudella

Andorra's national dish, escudella is a hearty stew made with meats (like pork, veal, or sausage), vegetables, pasta, and chickpeas. It's especially popular in winter and during festivals.

Trinxat

A traditional side dish or main made from mashed potatoes, cabbage, and garlic, often topped with pancetta or sausages. Think of it as the Pyrenean version of bubble and squeak.

Cargols a la llauna

Grilled snails seasoned with garlic, parsley, and olive oil, often cooked in a tin pan and served as a tapas style appetizer.

Xai Andorrà

Locally raised Andorran lamb, grilled or oven roasted, is a delicacy often served with mountain herbs and seasonal vegetables.

Formatge de tupí

A strong, fermented cheese spread aged in clay pots. It's typically eaten with crusty bread and a splash of liqueur.

Coca Massegada

A sweet, dry cake flavored with anise and lemon zest, commonly eaten for breakfast or dessert with coffee or sweet wine.

Seasonal Specialties

Wild mushrooms, game meats (boar, deer), and local trout are featured throughout the year depending on the season.

7.2 Top Restaurants and Local Favorites

From Michelin Rated dining rooms to traditional bordas, Andorra's restaurants combine fine cooking with charming settings. Here's a guide to the best dining experiences:

HighEnd and Fine Dining

Restaurant Borda Estevet (Andorra la Vella)

Located in a traditional stone house, this refined restaurant blends elegance with authenticity. Escudella and grilled meats are specialties.

Ibaya (Soldeu)
A Michelin Starred restaurant inside the Sport Hotel Hermitage. Expect a gourmet tasting menu with local ingredients reimagined in artistic presentations.

Restaurant Can Manel (Andorra la Vella)
Known for its grilled meats and traditional mountain cuisine, with top rated service and wine pairings.

MidRange Gems

La Borda de l'Avi (La Massana)
Rustic atmosphere and classic dishes like trinxat, slow roasted lamb, and hearty stews.

El Raco d'en Josep (Encamp)

Friendly, unpretentious, and family owned—great for enjoying Andorran comfort food.

Restaurant L'Ovella Negra (Canillo/Incles)
A mountain hideaway known for its atmosphere, seasonal menu, and fireside seating.

Hidden Local Spots

Borda Vella (Encamp)
Small, romantic, and perfect for couples seeking local flavors in a cozy, traditional setting.

Bar 66 (Ordino)
Casual and loved by locals—great for beer, snacks, and watching life go by in one of the prettiest villages.

7.3 Best Markets, Cafés & Street Eats

Eating well in Andorra doesn't always mean a formal restaurant experience. Local cafés and food markets give a more casual, authentic taste of Pyrenean flavors.

Food Markets

Mercat de la Vall (Andorra la Vella)
This weekend market offers everything from Andorran cheeses and sausages to handmade chocolates and honey.

Encamp Local Market
Seasonal and smaller in scale but great for fruits, cured meats, and artisan bread.

Café Culture

Café La Llum (Andorra la Vella)

A great place to unwind with coffee, pastries, and free WiFi. Popular among locals and remote workers.

Art i Pa (La Massana)
Bakery café known for its croissants, coffee, and relaxed vibe—perfect for a quiet morning.

Xocland (La Massana)
A chocolate café with handcrafted sweets, great coffee, and homemade desserts.

Street Eats and Casual Spots

Pizza Santa Anna (EscaldesEngordany)
Grab a pizza to go or dine casually with locals at this no frills spot with huge portions.

Creperie Les Delicies (Pas de la Casa)
Enjoy sweet and savory crepes in a ski village setting—great for families and aprèsski snacks.

Food Trucks at Festivals

During summer events or markets, you'll often find grilled sausages, churros, or even local cider being served from trucks or stalls.

7.4 Dietary Options: Vegan, GlutenFree, and More

Although Andorran cuisine is traditionally meatheavy, the country has evolved to accommodate modern dietary needs, especially in urban areas and ski resorts.

Vegan & Vegetarian Options

El Cantàbric (Andorra la Vella)
Offers vegetarian tapas and vegan options clearly marked on the menu.

The Family Room (La Massana)
Great spot with vegetarian and vegan bowls, salads, and soups made with local produce.

Vegetalia Supermarket

Organic and health food store that stocks vegan cheeses, gluten free snacks, and nondairy options.

GlutenFree Dining

Many restaurants now offer gluten free alternatives, especially in tourist hubs like Soldeu and Escaldes.

Cal Sinquede (Ordino) is one of the few places where glutenfree is more than an afterthought.

Hotels like Hotel Spa Termes Carlemany offer gluten free menus upon request.

Food Allergies & Language Tips

Catalan and Spanish are the most commonly used languages on menus. "Sense gluten" (glutenfree), "vegetarià" (vegetarian), and "vegà" (vegan) are good words to know.

Don't hesitate to ask staff directly—many restaurants are used to dietary questions due to the influx of international visitors.

Andorra may be small, but it boasts a surprisingly rich and varied food scene. From rustic stews shared in mountain lodges to contemporary vegan meals and world class dining, you'll never go hungry in this Pyrenean paradise. The key is knowing where to look and embracing the local ingredients and seasonal rhythms that define Andorran cuisine.

Chapter 8

Culture, History & Local Life

Andorra is more than a scenic mountain escape—it's a nation with a rich cultural identity shaped by centuries of isolation, resilience, and cross cultural influence. Nestled in the Pyrenees between France and Spain, this microstate has preserved distinct customs, folklore, and traditions that offer travelers a deeper, more meaningful experience. Whether you attend a vibrant festival, wander through Romanesque churches, or chat with locals in a stone village, Andorra's soul is found in its history and people.

8.1 Folklore, Festivals & National Holidays

Andorra's calendar is peppered with vibrant festivals and folklore events that blend Catholic traditions, seasonal rituals, and rural customs. Many of these celebrations have been passed down for generations and still unite entire communities today.

Major Festivals

Carnaval (February/March)
A preLenten celebration marked by costume parades, music, and masked balls. Each parish has its own version, with Andorra la Vella and Encamp hosting the largest events.

Sant Jordi (April 23)
Inspired by the Catalan tradition, this is Andorra's own version of Valentine's Day. Expect to see bookstalls, roses, poetry readings, and romantic street markets.

La Festa Major (July–September)

Each parish holds its own multi day summer fair, featuring dancing, fireworks, folk performances, and traditional Andorran games. Don't miss the one in Ordino for its authentic charm.

Meritxell Day (September 8)

Andorra's national holiday honors Our Lady of Meritxell, the country's patron saint. It includes religious processions, cultural exhibitions, and family picnics.

Traditional Elements

Dance of the Marratxi (La Massana)

A folk dance with mysterious origins, performed during major feasts wearing period costumes.

Buners (bagpipes) and traditional flutes often accompany community celebrations, keeping musical traditions alive.

Falles (torch processions) are lit on midsummer night, particularly during Sant Joan (June 23–24), a fiery and mystical ritual celebrating the summer solstice.

8.2 Andorra's Language, Religion & Traditions

Despite its size, Andorra has cultivated a strong cultural identity rooted in language, religion, and customs that reflect both isolation and openness.

Language

Catalan is the official language and a strong symbol of national pride.

Spanish and French are widely spoken, especially in tourism and business.

English is increasingly understood in resorts and shops, but learning a few Catalan phrases is appreciated.

Religion

Andorra is predominantly Roman Catholic, and churches play an important role in both religious and cultural life.

While secularism has grown, traditional religious holidays and customs remain significant.

Traditional Life

Andorran families have historically been self-sufficient, relying on farming, shepherding, and craftsmanship.

In rural areas, you may still see traditional bordes—stone barns or houses built with slate roofs, once used for livestock or storing hay.

Hospitality, respect for nature, and tight knit communities define the Andorran way of life.

Weddings & Ceremonies

Traditional Andorran weddings blend Catholic and rural customs, often celebrated over several days.

Many villages celebrate local saints and patron feasts with parades and church services that bring entire communities together.

8.3 Historic Sites and Churches to Explore

Andorra is a living museum of Romanesque architecture, with over 40 historic churches and numerous ancient structures that reflect centuries of faith, resilience, and art.

MustVisit Historic Sites

Sant Joan de Caselles (Canillo)

One of Andorra's most iconic Romanesque churches (11th century), known for its stone bell tower and 12th century frescoes.

Santa Coloma Church (Santa Coloma d'Andorra)

Features the oldest surviving preRomanesque structure in the country and houses a circular bell tower unique in the Pyrenees.

Casa de la Vall (Andorra la Vella)

A 16th century stone house that served as the seat of the General Council, Andorra's parliament. A symbol of the country's long standing democracy.

La Margineda Bridge

A medieval stone bridge on the outskirts of the capital, built in the 12th century—perfect for photos and a peaceful walk.

Other Notable Churches

Sant Martí de la Cortinada (La Cortinada)

Famous for its 17th century murals and baroque altarpiece.

Església de Sant Miquel d'Engolasters (Engolasters)

Offers incredible views and a glimpse into mountain worship sites dating back to the 12th century.

Local History Tip

Most churches are free to visit, and several are illuminated at night for dramatic effect. Guided tours and audio guides are available in Catalan, Spanish, French, and English.

8.4 Art Galleries, Museums & Cultural Centers

Andorra balances its historic charm with a growing modern art and cultural scene. Whether you're interested in sculpture, photography, or ethnographic history, the country has a diverse array of small but rich museums and creative hubs.

Top Museums

Museu Nacional de l'Automòbil (Encamp)
A surprise favorite, showcasing vintage cars and motorbikes from the early 20th century. A fun visit for all ages.

Casa Rull Museum (La Massana)
Explore rural life through the preserved home of a 19th century farming family.

Museu del Tabac (Sant Julià de Lòria)
Housed in an old tobacco factory, this museum tells the story of Andorra's agricultural and industrial heritage.

Centre d'Art d'Escaldes Engordany
Dedicated to Catalan modernism and local artists, with rotating exhibits and workshops.

Art Galleries & Cultural Spaces

Galeria Pilar Riberaygua (Andorra la Vella)
A contemporary gallery showcasing Andorran and international visual art.

Fàbrica Reig Cultural Center
A converted factory offering interactive exhibitions, performances, and educational programs.

LAndart Outdoor Art Exhibition
Held every two years in natural landscapes, blending environmental themes with modern art installations.

Cultural Events

Andorra la Vella Jazz Festival (July): Free outdoor concerts featuring jazz and world music.

Temporada de Teatre: A theater season running across the parishes, often featuring Catalan and international plays.

Andorra's cultural landscape is as rich and layered as its mountain valleys. Whether you're attending a village festival, admiring centuries old frescoes, or walking across a medieval bridge, every corner of the country has a story to tell. Immerse yourself in local life—not just by observing, but by participating, asking, and exploring.

Chapter 9

Outdoor Adventures & Nature Escapes

Andorra is an outdoor lover's dream. With more than 90% of the country covered in mountains, forests, lakes, and rivers, it's no wonder the Pyrenean microstate has become a haven for hikers, skiers, bikers, and nature seekers. Whether blanketed in snow or blooming with alpine wildflowers, Andorra offers year round excitement for every adventurer. This chapter explores the top outdoor activities across the seasons, from adrenaline sports to serene eco experiences.

9.1 Hiking Trails and National Parks

Andorra's well marked trail network spans hundreds of kilometers, with routes suited to casual walkers, seasoned trekkers, and families alike. Whether you want to summit rugged peaks or follow a tranquil river path, there's a trail for you.

MadriuPerafitaClaror Valley (UNESCO World Heritage Site)

Spanning over 42,000 acres, this glacial valley is Andorra's most iconic natural area and the country's only UNESCOlisted site.

Trails lead through ancient shepherd paths, stone huts, high meadows, and glacier formed lakes, offering incredible views and cultural history.

Coma Pedrosa Natural Park

Home to Andorra's highest peak (Coma Pedrosa at 2,942m), this park is a hiker's paradise with steep ascents, alpine flora, and cascading streams.

Recommended trails include Arinsal to Estanys de Montmantell, and the full day climb to the summit for experienced hikers.

Sorteny Valley Nature Park

Known for its biodiversity and family friendly routes, this eastern valley features botanical trails, picnic areas, and gentle walks ideal for all ages.

Over 700 species of flowers and plants can be found here, especially vibrant in spring and summer.

Ruta del Ferro (Iron Route)

A unique cultural nature trail tracing Andorra's historic ironworks industry.

Easy, informative walk through La Massana with art installations and restored buildings from the 17th century.

Hiking Tip: Trails are color coded (green for easy, blue for moderate, red/black for difficult) and can be followed using the "Active Tourism Andorra" app, which includes GPS navigation and maps.

9.2 Skiing, Snowboarding & Winter Fun

Andorra transforms into a snow sports playground each winter, attracting visitors from around the world to its world class ski resorts, snow parks, and cozy aprèsski culture.

Grandvalira

The largest ski domain in the Pyrenees with over 210 km of slopes, Grandvalira connects the parishes of Encamp, Canillo, El Tarter, Soldeu, Grau Roig, and Pas de la Casa.

Perfect for all levels: from beginner friendly slopes to black diamond runs, and freestyle zones for snowboarders.

Offers night skiing, ski schools, snowmobile tours, and igloo villages.

Vallnord – Pal Arinsal

Located near La Massana, Vallnord is great for families and intermediate skiers, with 63 km of trails, snowshoe paths, and a snow park.

Offers adaptive skiing programs, making it one of the most inclusive resorts in Europe.

Naturland (formerly Naturlandia)

Focused on eco-friendly and family winter activities: snow tubing, cross country skiing, snow biking, and the Tobotronc, the world's longest alpine coaster.

More Winter Fun

Heliskiing and freeride zones for expert adventurers.

Ski touring (randonée) is increasingly popular, allowing backcountry access to untouched snowfields.

Snowshoeing trails throughout the Madriu Valley and Sorteny for serene exploration.

Winter Tip: The ski season typically runs from early December to midApril, and lift passes are best purchased in advance online for discounts.

9.3 Summer Sports: Mountain Biking & Climbing

When the snow melts, Andorra becomes a summer sports mecca. The rugged terrain and highaltitude trails attract outdoor athletes and thrillseekers from around the world.

Mountain Biking

Andorra is one of Europe's top mountain biking destinations, hosting World Cup downhill events.

Vallnord Bike Park (Pal Arinsal) offers 25+ downhill and enduro trails, with lifts adapted for bikes.

Grandvalira Mountain Bike Park has trails ranging from beginner to pro, with rental and instruction available.

Road Cycling

Legendary routes that attract cyclists from the Tour de France and La Vuelta.

Popular climbs include Coll d'Ordino, Coll de la Gallina, and Port d'Envalira—Europe's highest paved pass.

Great for endurance training and scenic views.

Rock Climbing & Via Ferrata

Over 20 via ferrata routes, iron assisted climbs with cables, ladders, and fixed anchors, allow safe access to sheer mountain faces.

Clot de l'Aspra (Sant Julià) and Roc d'Esquerres (Escaldes) are popular sites.

Adventure Parks

Mon(t) Magic Family Park (Canillo) has ziplines, rope bridges, archery, and water activities for kids and adults.

Vertical adventures such as canyoning, paragliding, and guided high altitude trekking are offered by local outfitters.

Summer Tip: Most adventure parks open from June to September, and guided excursions are available in English, French, and Spanish.

9.4 Wildlife Watching and EcoTours

Nature lovers will be thrilled by Andorra's unique biodiversity, protected in its national parks and remote valleys. Spotting wildlife, birds, and alpine flora is both accessible and rewarding.

Wildlife You Might See

Pyrenean chamois (isard) – agile mountain goats often seen on rocky ridges.

Marmots – cute, burrowing creatures commonly seen (and heard!) on high altitude trails.

Bearded vultures (lammergeier) – enormous birds that soar above cliffs, part of Andorra's conservation efforts.

Red deer, wild boars, foxes, and other mammals are found deeper in the forests.

Birdwatching

Sorteny and Coma Pedrosa Parks are ideal for observing golden eagles, owls, woodpeckers, and migratory birds.

Specialized ecotours and photography outings are available.

EcoTours and Nature Walks

Local guides offer interpretive nature walks that focus on medicinal plants, geology, and ecosystems.

Some hotels and lodges partner with ecotourism agencies to offer sustainable experiences that support local conservation.

Stargazing

Andorra's high altitude villages and valleys make for excellent stargazing conditions.

Attend a night hike or astronomy event organized by Parc Natural de Sorteny or Grandvalira's observation stations.

EcoTip: Many protected areas limit access during mating seasons or harsh weather. Always follow marked paths and respect local wildlife.

From snow covered peaks to sundrenched forests, Andorra delivers a fourseason adventure in every sense. Whether you're chasing speed, searching for silence, or simply looking to breathe cleaner air and touch the clouds, this chapter proves that the real treasure of Andorra lies outdoors.

Chapter 10

Practical Travel Essentials

As your Andorran adventure draws near, preparation is just as important as excitement. This chapter is your goto toolkit for navigating daytoday logistics in the country. From managing money and staying connected to handling emergencies and using helpful travel apps, we've packed this section with real world advice to help make your trip smooth, safe, and stress free. Whether you're a first time visitor or a returning traveler, these essentials will set you up for success in Europe's mountain gem.

10.1 Currency, Budgeting & DutyFree Shopping

Currency Used in Andorra

Although Andorra is not an EU member, it uses the euro (€) as its de facto official currency.

Credit and debit cards (Visa, MasterCard, Maestro) are widely accepted in cities and ski resorts.

Always carry some cash for rural areas, small shops, or mountain lodges where cards may not be accepted.

Budgeting for Your Trip

Budget Travelers (€50–€80/day):
Stay in hostels or guesthouses, eat at cafés, and use public transport.

MidRange Travelers (€100–€180/day):
Enjoy boutique hotels, occasional fine dining, and excursions like spas or guided hikes.

Luxury Travelers (€200+/day):
4–5 star hotels, private ski instructors, spa treatments, and fine wine dining.

Sample costs:

Meal at a local restaurant: €12–€20

Ski day pass (Grandvalira): €50–€60

Bus ticket within a parish: €1.90–€3

Souvenir (artisan goods, handmade): €10–€40

DutyFree Shopping: What to Know

Andorra is a shopping haven thanks to its low taxes and duty free status, attracting visitors from France and Spain.

Popular items include alcohol, tobacco, electronics, cosmetics, and fashion.

Top shopping zones: Avinguda Meritxell (Andorra la Vella) and Carlemany Avenue (Escaldes Engordany).

Limits apply at borders, so know your duty free allowances before returning to the EU:

1L spirits OR 2L wine

200 cigarettes

Goods up to €900 in value per adult (€450 for minors)

Shopping Tip: Check for the TaxFree symbol. Visitors from outside the EU can sometimes reclaim VAT depending on the shop.

10.2 Safety, Emergency Services & Healthcare

Andorra is one of Europe's safest countries, with a low crime rate and an excellent healthcare system. Still, travelers should know how to handle emergencies or medical issues.

General Safety

Pickpocketing and scams are rare but can occur in busy shopping streets—stay alert in tourist zones.

Mountain safety is crucial: check weather conditions before hikes or drives.

Trails are generally well marked, but don't go off track in winter without a guide or avalanche training.

Emergency Numbers

General emergency: 112

Police (Andorran Police Service): +376 872 000

Fire Department: +376 873 100

Ambulance/Medical Emergency: +376 861 000

All emergency services respond in Catalan, Spanish, French, and English.

Hospitals & Clinics

Hospital Nostra Senyora de Meritxell (EscaldesEngordany) is the country's main medical center, equipped for emergencies.

Private clinics and dental centers are also available in urban areas.

Travel Insurance Tip: Always travel with valid insurance that covers mountain sports, accidents, and medical evacuation if needed.

10.3 SIM Cards, WiFi & Staying Connected

Staying connected in Andorra requires some planning, especially since Andorra is not part of EU roaming agreements, meaning international roaming charges can apply, even for EU visitors.

Getting a SIM Card

Local SIM cards are sold under Andorra Telecom, the country's only provider.

Available at official stores in Andorra la Vella, Escaldes, Pas de la Casa, and some tourist hubs.

Prepaid packages range from €10 to €30 with data only or combo voice/data plans.

Requires passport ID to register.

WiFi Access

Free WiFi hotspots are common in:

Hotels and accommodations

Restaurants and ski lodges

Public libraries and government buildings

Grandvalira and Vallnord resorts also offer limited free WiFi at base stations and cafés.

Connection Tip: Use messaging apps (WhatsApp, Telegram, Signal) for most communication, as voice calls via roaming can be expensive.

10.4 Travel Apps, Maps & Local Contacts

Traveling smart in Andorra means making use of modern tools and local knowledge. Here are some essential digital and offline resources.

MustHave Travel Apps

Visit Andorra (official app): Events, trails, webcams, weather updates, and attractions.

Andorra Bus: Real Time bus schedules, routes, and ticket booking.

AllTrails or Wikiloc: Excellent for mapping hikes and tracking progress in rural areas.

Moovit or Rome2Rio: Great for navigating intercity routes from Barcelona or Toulouse into Andorra.

Offline Maps & GPS

Download Google Maps offline for Andorra before arrival.

Maps.me is a great offline map alternative with trail routes.

Tourist information centers provide paper maps—great for remote zones with weak signals.

Local Contacts

Tourist Information Offices are located in Andorra la Vella, Encamp, Pas de la Casa, and Ordino.

Staff speak multiple languages and can assist with lodging, transit, and emergencies.

Embassy Services: Andorra doesn't host embassies but is served by:

French Embassy in Andorra: +376 871 500

Spanish Consulate in Andorra: +376 807 040

Local Tip: Always carry a hotel business card or address when venturing out—especially helpful when language is a barrier or phone battery dies.

With your essentials in place—money sorted, SIM card secured, maps loaded, and emergency contacts handy—you're fully equipped to enjoy Andorra with confidence. This chapter ties together everything you need to travel smart and savor your adventure, whether you're tackling the slopes, hiking high passes, or exploring ancient valleys.

Printed in Dunstable, United Kingdom